MILTON AVERY

MILTON AVERY

MILTON

AVERY

PRINTS AND DRAWINGS

1930–1964

Designed, printed and distributed for The Brooklyn Museum
by Shorewood Publishers, Inc., New York City

Text by

UNA E. JOHNSON

Curator of Prints and Drawings
The Brooklyn Museum

Commemorative Essay by
MARK ROTHKO

Monograph No. 4 in the series:

AMERICAN GRAPHIC ARTISTS OF THE TWENTIETH CENTURY,

published by The Brooklyn Museum under a grant from
The Ford Foundation Program in Humanities and the Arts

ACKNOWLEDGMENTS

Special acknowledgments are made to Mrs. Milton Avery, who not only made available most of Milton Avery's original works but also supplied otherwise unavailable information; and to Mr. Mark Rothko for graciously permitting the publication of his commemorative essay on Milton Avery.

Acknowledgments are extended also to Mr. and Mrs. Warren Brandt, Mr. Sylvan Cole, Mr. and Mrs. Budd Hopkins, Mr. and Mrs. Hans Moller, and Mr. Roy Neuberger.

INTRODUCTION

M ILTON AVERY belongs to that rare and gifted company of artists whose vision of humanity and art is large enough to transform the ordinary events of life into a universal visual poetry. Avery was not an innovator; for him it was of greater importance that the eye and hand be able to capture the essence of a scene through paintings and prints. He chose to hold, in time and space, the immediate retinal image of mountains and sea, and of figures at work or leisure within such landscapes. His wife, his daughter and his friends made up the repertory of images to which he gave a subtle geniality and casual humor. A perceptive eye and integrity of vision served him well. His skilled hand set down — in countless paintings, drawings, watercolors, some 200 monotypes and 48 prints — a gay, sometimes nostalgic chronicle of his experiences.

Milton Avery was born March 7, 1893, in the small village of Altmar in upper New York State where his father worked as a tanner. When he was twelve, the Avery family moved to Hartford, Connecticut. It was there, at the Connecticut League of Art Students, that he received his brief formal training in art. However, this sketchy training was sufficient to commit him to the life of a painter. In 1925, at the age of 32, he came to New York and his active career as an artist dates from that time. New York galleries offered a profusion of visual experiences through paintings of various periods and styles. Here he first saw the dazzling achievements of French painting: the Impressionists, the Post Impressionists, especially Gauguin and Bonnard, and the new work of Matisse and Braque. This same year he spent several months at Gloucester, Massachusetts which was a popular summer art colony of the 1920's and '30's. During this pleasant sojourn he met a young painter and illustrator, Sally Michel, also from New York, whom he married a year later.

Thus began a long and happy domestic life that provided many subjects for Avery's creative work. Portraits of his wife, his daughter, and fellow artists, their travels to the mountains and the sea, from the Gaspé Peninsula to Florida, to California and to Mexico. Sally Avery's devotion to Milton Avery was constant and beneficial. She allowed nothing to interfere with his work and his development as an artist. Her understanding and enjoyment of his creativity, gay wit and poetic vision sustained them both even in the lean and discouraging years of the 1930's. Their life, with their wide circle of friends, was a saga of warmth, work and mutual respect. In reality, the efforts of two artists forged the enchantment of Milton Avery's work — his own and Sally's. When he became discouraged at the slowness of recognition and the meagerness of financial returns, as did many American artists during that decade, Sally consoled and encouraged him. Avery's commitment as an artist was always unhampered. And he himself never permitted irritation and frustration to cloud his exuberant spirit.

Milton Avery was a keen draftsman to whom drawing was a necessity. His drawings done with felt-nibbed pen noted in *Dune Grasses,* 1959, and *Orchard in Bloom,* 1956, and the quick pen and ink sketch, *Sandspit and Birds,* 1957, are seemingly effortless accomplishments. Each line breaks easily and, at the right moment, flows as rhythmically as a heartbeat.

Over many years, the Averys and a small group of artist friends met regularly once a week to sketch from the model and to discuss the absorbing subject of picture making. In this, Avery held to the Renaissance point of view that the picture is of greater importance than merely painting it. It is further to be noted that in Avery's work a shy humor often conceals a sure intuition and sophistication.

Avery's drawings reveal his abiding interest in the figure itself rather than in its fleeting spatial motion. His apparently casual compositions have a disciplined grace and order. Their effortless quality is the result of long years of practice and careful observation. He executed hundreds of sketches and also kept many small notebooks in which are recorded brief and barely suggested compositions, with many color notations. It was from this source that Avery developed many of his drawings, watercolors, and monotypes.

Critics often compared Avery to Matisse and early in his career took him to task for following the French tradition too closely. For Bonnard, Matisse and Braque, style was a manner of being arrived at through long observation, experience and appropriate atmosphere. For Avery, this

8

was also true. This affinity may have isolated him from some fellow American artists to whom style was a manner of painting and represented little reflection and sometimes less experience. Perhaps the fundamental similarity between Matisse and Avery is their delight and excitement in the visual experience of drawing. They were both content to please the beholder, leaving problems to less exuberant talents.

The baroque imagery of Matisse so evident in floral patterns, stripes and checks and flowing arabesques often remains impersonal and intellectual. While Avery's drawings lack the analytical presentation of the French, they are still classic in their simplicity and warmth. It was through these major European influences that Avery's own style of drawing and painting emerged and grew. The French painters found no need to make overt reference to any social comment or obvious social cause. Such preoccupations also held little interest for Avery who by temperament and deep humility had a far wider vision. Rather, Avery was inclined to heed Thoreau's belief: "If a man does not keep pace with his companions, perhaps it is because he hears the beat of a different drummer. Let him step to the music which he hears, however measured or far away."[1]

Avery held to the essential elements of his subject with "English restraint." Many years later Sally Avery recalled that during their travels in England, the tall, spare, reticent figure of Milton Avery might have been almost any Englishman in London, in the small villages or coastal towns. This quality of restraint may be noted in all of Avery's work. It appears in the rising line of a hill that defines a high horizon, the suggested calligraphy of grasses, a tree, the regular movement of a wave, the curving hull of a boat, an umbrella, or distant sand dunes. Again the essential image is preserved in the wonderfully blotted ink drawing titled *Spotty Trees*, 1956. A spare intensity envelops Avery's graphic work and synthesized his own style which flowered with elegance and perceptiveness in the last decades of his work. It also serves to reemphasize the underlying reality of his endeavor to encompass on paper and canvas his own visual experiences. The ease with which Avery draws the figure is to be noted in the early composition entitled *Sleeping Girl*, 1930, in the more direct and greatly simplified drawing *Three Figures* of 1950 and in the *Recumbent Nude* of 1962. Among the many portrait studies, the 1959 *Self-Portrait* is unusual in its heavily patterned composition which still retains its characteristic directness and intensity.

---

1. Thoreau, Henry David. *Walden and Other Writings*, New York, 1950, p. 290

It has been pointed out that Avery grew up as a painter in the days of the "American scene" movement.[2] This self conscious, somewhat turgid movement came into being soon after that impressive Mexican development in modern mural painting which gave a new dimension to 20th century painting in the Western Hemisphere. The movement thrived during a period when American painters often chose to ignore the European tradition. Its positive value was its forced consideration of American life and the spatial qualities of American landscape. Early in Milton Avery's student days, he had looked at the works of Albert Pinkham Ryder, Mary Cassatt, Childe Hassam and other American Impressionists. His interest was held by the immediacy of a scene and its momentary pattern and flatness of surface in which formal perspective played no part. He was not interested in volume or great masses and their corresponding forms. Avery himself said: "I always take something out of my pictures."[3] Again this was a striving for the essence of a particular image rather than a forced economy of means. "I strip the design to essentials; the facts do not interest me as much as the essence of nature." The artist continues: "I never have any rules to follow. I follow myself. I began painting by myself in the Connecticut countryside, always directly from nature. It was only after many years that I began to work from sketches. I never thought of being interested in pattern, but my work always stressed it."[4]

Beginning in 1950 and continuing through nearly ten years, Milton Avery executed approximately 200 monotypes mostly in oils but occasionally in far more difficult watercolors. A monotype is a single printed impression produced by painting a design on a plain, flat surface, usually glass or metal, and then transferring it to or literally blotting it onto a sheet of paper. This is a printing process similar to that of the hand pulled woodcut but dissimilar in that there is no incised or cut printing surface and only one clear impression is possible.

As far as may be ascertained the monotype came into being in the 17th century and is first recorded in the works of the Italian artist, Giovanni Castiglione. Perhaps the French•artist, Edgar Degas, in the late 19th century was the first to make extensive use of this special medium as a means of extending the elements of his own painting. It will be recalled

2. Greenberg, Clement. *Art and Culture. Critical Essays*, Boston, 1961, p. 197
3. Ritter, Chris. "A Milton Avery Profile." *The Art Digest*, XXVII (December 1, 1952), pp. 11-12
4. Ritter, Chris. Op. cit.

that the American artist, Maurice Prendergast, in the early 1900's also employed the medium in some 200 fine examples. To Avery it was a most auspicious medium for its softness of quality and the disciplined order of its color sequences. The resulting forms offered still another means of capturing the very essence of an image. It was a challenging medium because the picture either came off magnificently or it was a failure. Avery, as did Prendergast some fifty years before, considered his monotypes a special and important part of his total work. Many were formally exhibited in 1950 at the Laurel Gallery. The present monograph lists only a small number of the entire group. Avery's ability to depict the figure with his characteristic ease and in the basic simplicity of forms is to be noted in the splendid monotype, *Reclining Nudes*, 1950. The solid forms and their forthright presentation have the directness often seen in sculptors' drawings. The charming still life, *Leaves*, 1951, with its floating imagery, the almost mythical tree in the the freely rendered *Setting Sun*, 1951, have a fluency of style and warm personal vision of an artist whose eye and hand are combined to capture and hold a brief moment in time and space.

Milton Avery made his first drypoint plates in 1933 more as a happenstance than as a begining interest in printmaking itself. In the stringent years of the thirties, the expense of papers, canvas, brushes and paints, in other words the basic materials and tools necessary to an artist, were often a prohibitive tax on his dwindling budget. Avery processed his own canvas, used less elegant papers and painted with a less loaded brush, and on occasion thinned down his paint. In 1933, Sally Avery's sister brought into the Avery household some small irregular plates of polished copper and zinc. These were scraps discarded by a commercial engraving shop with which she had had business dealings. Using a pointed tool, Milton Avery opened up furry lines on the metal plate in the same manner that he made pen drawings. He had no thought of carrying out the mechanics of printing. In fact most of his plates were printed years after he had originally executed them. Perhaps Avery found in the resistance of the metal plate a new challenge to his draftsmanship. The thin smoky burr of the drypoint line also appealed to him. His drypoint plates carry the same subject matter as do his paintings. In fact they were often studies made after his paintings and were done as a change from a full day of painting.

Avery's first drypoint plates were two small sketches of his infant daughter, March. In 1934 he made a more ambitious plate entitled *My Wife*,

Sally, a composition made directly from a painting of two years earlier called *Woman with Green Face*. The subject is seated at a table, preoccupied with a sketch of her own. When the plate was printed the figure appeared left-handed merely because Avery had never considered the printed result. The following year Avery incised a large and more ambitious drypoint plate entitled *Young Girl Nude* in which a standing figure is placed before a sketchily outlined mirror and chest of drawers which serve as a flat background pattern. The straight uncompromising line of the left arm, the deliberate elongation of the legs produce an angular awkwardness at once knowing and naïve, traits often combined in Avery's work, giving it his special quality of enchantment.

Between 1936 and 1939, Avery ventured more definitely into portraiture with the drypoints, *Rothko with a Pipe, Self Portrait, Man with Pipe,* and *Sally with Beret,* the latter three rendered full-face. Strength, simplicity and ease of handling mark these perceptive studies. A measure of insight and wisdom give them a special aura. Also in 1939, Avery composed the small drypoint called *Japanese Landscape,* in which the essential form of the tree is bluntly drawn against the somewhat brief and staccato lines of the spare hills.

Two years later, in 1941, Avery set down on a copper plate one of his largest intaglio prints. Entitled *Standing Nude,* it is reminiscent of the earlier drypoint, *Young Girl Nude,* of 1935. However, in the later print the drypoint lines are strongly stroked and the upright lines accentuate and define the easy stance of the monumental female figure. A somewhat different subject is noted in the drypoint, *Window by the Sea,* also completed in 1941, where a single trailing branch of flowers is held gracefully in the severe lines of a window facing an open sea. The casual placement, balance, and understated imagery carry a singular grace.

Not until 1948 did Avery seriously consider the printing of his drypoint plates. At that time Chris Ritter, a friend of Avery's and the Director of the Laurel Gallery in New York City, selected five plates for one of the Laurel Portfolios. Ritter had organized the Laurel Gallery in 1946 to present contemporary American artists. As a means of introducing his artists to a wider public, Ritter offered original prints by each of them at five dollars a print or twenty-five dollars for a portfolio of five. One of Avery's prints had been included in the second group portfolio. The fourth Laurel portfolio was composed entirely of Avery's prints and issued in an edition of 100. The Portfolios were printed at Atelier 17 in New York under the direct supervision of Stanley William Hayter. Hayter's highly trained eye caught the freshness and elegance of Avery's drypoints and he printed them with all the perceptiveness and skill at his command. Although the portfolio contained five of Avery's finest prints, it was ignored and did not sell at the time of issue. The print entitled *By the Sea*, from this series, was a favored theme of Avery's. Some years later he returned to this theme in his small painting, *Umbrella by the Sea*, of 1951, and still later in a more abstract concept in two 1956 paintings, *Black Umbrella* and *Sea Gazers*. The drypoint, *Riders in the Park*, comes near to formal perspective in its diagonal thrust but basically remains a small graphic essay in patterns. The largest print in the portfolio is *Reclining Nude*, in which the artist defined the strong lithe contours of a single great figure through long, swinging strokes giving a sense of form and weight to the bold composition. Again the form is elongated and a single sharp angle arrests the attention and brings a wittily unexpected note to an otherwise sedate figure. The two remaining prints of the portfolio, *March at Table* and *Head of a Man*, further demonstrate the artist's keen vision and his ability to capture an expressive moment within a few exquisitely patterned forms. Each element of the composition falls into its rightful place with natural ease and simplicity.

The drypoint plate, *Head of March*, 1948, sometimes called *March with Babushka*, was acquired for the Collectors of American Art, an organization of individual collectors held together for many years by the active and enthusiastic direction of Emily A. Francis. This plate was printed in an edition of 100 at Hayter's Atelier 17 and issued to the membership in December, 1949. Its diamond shaped composition was a departure from the conventional rectangular form of Avery's other prints.

Head of March ended Avery's intaglio work save for one other drypoint, *Nude Combing Hair*, completed in 1961. Although it is similar to the 1941 drypoint, *Reclining Nude*, its lines are less direct and the long curves are arrested by a tacky accent. The major part of Avery's graphic work was executed between 1933 and 1948 and included 26 prints. However, a large number of Avery's plates were not printed until much later, in 1964, when Sally Avery took them to the skilled printers, Andersen Lamb Photogravure Corporation, located at the foot of the Brooklyn Bridge. Impressions were printed in editions of 20, 60 or 100. Each print was signed and numbered by the artist.

Avery did not return to prints again until 1952. This time he worked in the broad flat forms of the woodcut. Between 1953 and 1955 he made 19 relief prints which in composition also are similar to his paintings. Mainly in black and white, they occasionally are printed with a solid background color of blue, yellow, brown and red. *Fantail Pigeon,* 1953, was printed with brown and a blue background, although the black-and-white version seems more effective as a woodcut. The woodcut *Lamb,* 1954, is a small but simplified version of a 1952 painting entitled *Sheep.* The repeated motif of flying sea birds in the woodcut *Birds and Sea,* completed in 1955, is reminiscent of a painting called *Flight,* of a year earlier. The woodcuts are in editions averaging from 15 to 100 impressions and bring Avery's total graphic work of monotypes, drypoints and relief prints to nearly 250 subjects.

Two major themes dominate the extensive work of Milton Avery: the figure, and views of landscape and sea. His figures, often abstract in their economy of means, are sometimes devoid of facial expression. Nevertheless, they remain completely individual personalities. His landscapes are not just any landscapes but have the bewitching quality of recalling to each observer a particular landscape. Avery was concerned with the elements that make up time and space. The immediacy of the moment is captured and translated into a few significant lines and simple forms that holds the essence of a blithe and poetic vision.

Perhaps, in the final analysis, among the most gratifying rewards of an artist is the whole-hearted recognition of his work by his fellow artists. Milton Avery reaped this in warmth and abundance. His work, his ideas about painting and about life were recognized and highly respected not only by the artists of his generation but by avant-garde artists of the succeeding generation, regardless of what style they themselves pursued. Among such friends were Mark Rothko, Adolph Gottlieb, Paul Bodin, Stephen Pace, and Alex Katz. There were many others who knew him and who often treasured a small sketch or watercolor which they had either received from Avery or purchased for their own enjoyment. During a long and productive lifetime, Milton Avery pursued the illustrious but demanding art of painting and drawing with enormous zeal and not a little enchantment.

UNA E. JOHNSON

14

COMMEMORATIVE ESSAY

by

MARK ROTHKO

I would like to say a few words about the greatness of Milton Avery.

This conviction of greatness, the feeling that one was in the presence of great events, was immediate on encountering his work. It was true for many of us who were younger, questioning, and looking for an anchor. This conviction has never faltered. It has persisted, and has been reinforced through the passing decades and the passing fashions.

I cannot tell you what it meant for us during those early years to be made welcome in those memorable studios on Broadway, 72nd Street, and Columbus Avenue. We were, there, both the subjects of his paintings and his idolatrous audience. The walls were always covered with an endless and changing array of poetry and light.

The instruction, the example, the nearness in the flesh of this marvelous man — all this was a significant fact — one which I shall never forget.

Avery is first a great poet. His is the poetry of sheer loveliness, of sheer beauty. Thanks to him this kind of poetry has been able to survive in our time.

This — alone — took great courage in a generation which felt that it could be heard only through clamor, force and a show of power. But Avery had that inner power in which gentleness and silence proved more audible and poignant.

From the beginning there was nothing tentative about Avery. He always had that naturalness, that exactness and that inevitable completeness which can be achieved only by those gifted with magical means, by those born to sing.

15

There have been several others in our generation who have celebrated the world around them, but none with that inevitability where the poetry penetrated every pore of the canvas to the very last touch of the brush. For Avery was a great poet-inventor who had invented sonorities never seen nor heard before. From these we have learned much and will learn more for a long time to come.

What was Avery's repertoire? His living room, Central Park, his wife Sally, his daughter March, the beaches and mountains where they summered; cows, fish heads, the flight of birds; his friends and whatever world strayed through his studio: a domestic, unheroic cast. But from these there have been fashioned great canvases, that far from the casual and transitory implications of the subjects, have always a gripping lyricism, and often achieve the permanence and monumentality of Egypt.

I grieve for the loss of this great man. I rejoice for what he has left us.

Memorial Address delivered at
The New York Society for Ethical Culture
2 West 64 Street on January 7, 1965

CATALOGUE

Dimensions are listed in inches with height preceding width. Measurements of intaglio prints are those of the plate mark; sheet size is given for drawings and monotypes. Works are listed chronologically, alphabetized within each year. Only a representative group of drawings has been listed.

Full editions of the complete series of intaglio prints were printed in 1964 by the Andersen Lamb Photogravure Corporation in Brooklyn. The artist meticulously numbered his editions, which range from 20 to 118, and signed them in pencil.

Research by
JO MILLER
Assistant Curator of Prints and Drawings
The Brooklyn Museum

DRAWINGS

1. SLEEPING GIRL, 1930
   Steel pen and ink, 11⅛ x 14⅛
   Signed "Milton Avery," lower right
   Collection of Mrs. Milton Avery

2. DOLIA, 1946
   Ink (felt-tipped pen), 16⅞ x 13⅞
   Signed "Milton Avery 1946,"
   center left
   Collection of Mrs. Milton Avery

3. *a.* MOUNTAINS, 1947, blue ink
   b. PINES, 1947, ink (felt-tipped pen)
   Two drawings on one sheet, 16 x 13
   Signed "Milton Avery," lower right
   Collection of Mrs. Milton Avery

4. NUDE WITH NET, 1949
   Ink, 14 x 17
   Collection of Mr. and Mrs.
   Warren Brandt

5. NUDE WITH PILLOW, 1949
   Ink, 16½ x 14
   Collection of Mr. and Mrs.
   Warren Brandt

6. THREE FIGURES, 1950
   Ink (felt-tipped pen), 13½ x 16½
   Signed "Milton Avery 1950,"
   lower right
   Collection of Mr. and Mrs.
   Budd Hopkins

7. *a.* TREE, 1951, ink
   (felt-tipped pen)
   b. TREES, 1951, ink
   (felt-tipped pen)
   Two drawings on one sheet, 11 x 8½
   Signed "Milton Avery 1951,"
   lower right
   Collection of Mrs. Milton Avery

8. WORRIED WIFE, 1951
   Ink and pencil, 11 x 8½
   Signed "Milton Avery 1951,"
   lower right
   Collection of Mrs. Milton Avery

9. NUDE, 1953
   Ink (felt-tipped pen), 17 x 14
   Signed "Milton Avery 1953,"
   lower right
   Collection of Mr. and Mrs.
   Hans Moller

10. ORCHARD IN BLOOM, 1956
    Ink (felt-tipped pen), 8½ x 11
    Signed "Milton Avery," center right
    Collection of Mrs. Milton Avery

11. SPOTTY TREES, 1956
    Ink, 17¾ x 24
    Signed "Milton Avery," lower right
    Collection of Mrs. Milton Avery

12. THREE WOMEN, 1956
    Ink (felt-tipped pen), 16⅞ x 13⅞
    Signed "Milton Avery 1956,"
    lower left
    Collection of Mrs. Milton Avery

13. TWO NUDES, 1956
    Crayon, pencil and pen, 17 x 14
    Signed "Milton Avery 1956,"
    lower right
    Collection of Mr. and Mrs.
    Philip Cavanaugh

14. TWO NUDES, 1956
Ink (felt-tipped pen), 16⅞ x 13⅞
Signed "Milton Avery 1956,"
    lower left
Collection of Mrs. Milton Avery

15. SANDSPIT AND BIRDS, 1957
Ink (felt-tipped pen), 8½ x 11
Signed "Milton Avery," lower right
Collection of Mrs. Milton Avery

16. SOARING GULL, 1957
Charcoal and watercolor wash,
    20 x 26
Signed "Milton Avery 1957,"
    lower right
Collection of Mrs. Milton Avery

17. TANGLED TREES, 1957
Ink (felt-tipped pen), 8½ x 11
Signed "Milton Avery 1957,"
    lower right
Collection of Mrs. Milton Avery

18. RECLINING NUDE ON
    BLANKET, 1958
Crayon and ink, 16¾ x 13¾
*Collection of Donald Morriss Gallery,
    Detroit*
Reproduced in *One Hundred
    Contemporary American Drawings,*
    The University of Michigan
    Museum of Art, 1965, No. 4

19. ROUGH SEA, 1958
Ink (felt-tipped pen), 6 x 8⅜
Signed "1958 Milton Avery,"
    lower right
Collection of Mrs. Milton Avery

20. COWS ON HILLSIDE, 1959
Ink (felt-tipped pen), 4⅞ x 8½
Signed "Milton Avery 1959,"
    lower right
Collection of Mrs. Milton Avery

21. DUNE GRASSES, 1959
Ink (felt-tipped pen), 6 x 8½
Signed "Milton Avery 1959,"
    lower left-center
*Collection of Mr. and Mrs.
    Philip Cavanaugh*

22. SELF-PORTRAIT, 1959
Ink (felt-tipped pen), 11 x 8½
Signed "Milton Avery 1959,"
    lower right
Collection of Mrs. Milton Avery

23. TENDER DUNES, 1960
Pen, ink and pencil, 8½ x 11
Signed "Milton Avery 1960,"
    lower left
Collection of Mrs. Milton Avery

24. RECUMBENT NUDE, 1962
Ink (felt-tipped pen), 16¼ x 21½
Signed "Milton Avery 1962,"
    lower left
Collection of Mrs. Milton Avery

25. ARTIST AND MODEL, n.d.
Ink (felt-tipped pen), 16⅞ x 13⅞
Signed "Milton Avery," lower left
Collection of Mrs. Milton Avery

26. NUDE RECLINING, n.d.
Blue ink and crayon, 16⅞ x 13⅞
Signed "Milton Avery," lower right
*Collection of Mr. and Mrs.
    Philip Cavanaugh*

27. SEA GULLS AND SEA, n.d.
Ink (felt-tipped pen), 13⅞ x 16⅞
Signed "Milton Avery," lower right
Collection of Mrs. Milton Avery

28. SEATED WOMAN, n.d.
Blue ink, 16⅞ x 13⅞
Signed "Milton Avery," lower right
Collection of Mrs. Milton Avery

29. UNTITLED (Three Seated Nude
    Figures), n.d.
    Ink (felt-tipped pen), 8¼ x 11
    Inscribed "Greetings to My Dear
    Friend Roy On this his Birthday,"
    lower center
    Signed "Milton Avery," lower left
    Collection of Mr. Roy Neuberger

MONOTYPES

*All of the following monotypes are in the
collection of Mrs. Milton Avery. All are in
oil, unless noted otherwise.*

30. ARTIST'S CHILD, 1950
    Monotype (watercolor), 22 x 17
    Signed "Milton Avery," lower left

31. BOWL OF FRUIT, 1950
    Monotype, 22 x 17
    Signed "Milton Avery,"
    on bowl in composition

32. BUST, 1950
    Monotype, 22 x 17
    Signed "Milton Avery," lower left

33. FEMALE ARTIST, 1950
    Monotype, 22 x 17
    Signed "Milton Avery," lower left

34. GRECIAN HEAD, 1950
    Monotype, 22 x 17
    Signed "Milton Avery," lower right

35. NUDE SEATED, 1950
    Monotype, 22 x 17
    Signed "Milton Avery," lower right

36. PROUD HEN, 1950
    Monotype, 18 x 24
    Signed "Milton Avery," lower right

37. RECLINING NUDES, 1950
    Monotype, 17 x 22
    Signed "Milton Avery," lower left

38. WOMAN WITH BERET, 1950
    Monotype, 17 x 22
    Signed "Milton Avery," lower right

39. BIRD IN FLIGHT, 1951
    Monotype, 18 x 24
    Signed "Milton Avery," lower left

40. FLOWERING PLANT, 1951
    Monotype, 17 x 22
    Signed "Milton Avery," lower right

41. LEAVES, 1951
    Monotype, 22 x 17
    Signed "Milton Avery 1951,"
    on vase in composition

42. PELICAN, 1951
    Monotype, 17 x 22
    Signed "Milton Avery," lower right

43. POND AND PALMS, 1951
    Monotype, 12 x 18
    Signed "Milton Avery," lower left

44. RECLINING NUDE, 1951
    Monotype, 18 x 25⅛
    Signed "Milton Avery." lower center

SELF-PORTRAIT, 1951
Monotype, 18 x 24
Signed "Milton Avery," lower left

SETTING SUN, 1951
Monotype, 18 x 24
Signed "Milton Avery," lower left

SPRING IN NEW HAMPSHIRE,
1954
Monotype, 18 x 24
Signed "Milton Avery," lower right

FUNNY HORSE, 1955
Monotype (watercolor), 17 x 22
Signed "Milton Avery," lower left

LOVELY TREE, 1956
Monotype (watercolor), 23⅝ x 17¾
Signed "Milton Avery," lower left

SOLITARY TREE, 1956
Monotype, 23½ x 17⅞
Signed "Milton Avery," lower left

PRINTS

1. BABY AVERY, 1933
Drypoint, 8⅞ x 5⅞
Edition: 60

2. SLEEPING BABY, 1933
Drypoint, 5⅜ x 7⅝
Edition: 100
Reproduced in *Artist's Proof,*
Vol. III, No. 5, Spring–summer,
1963, p. 29

53. MY WIFE SALLY, 1934
Drypoint, 5⅜ x 7⅝
Edition: 100
Note: After a painting, *Woman with
Green Face,* 1932, in the Collection
of Mr. and Mrs. Gustave Kellner

54. YOUNG GIRL NUDE, 1935
Drypoint, 9⅞ x 4½
Edition: 100

55. CHILD CUTTING, 1936
Drypoint, 5⅛ x 6¾
Edition: 100
Reproduced in *Milton Avery.
Etchings and Woodcuts,*
Associated American Artists,
1963, No. 5

56. DRAWBRIDGE, 1936
Drypoint, 6¼ x 12¾
Edition: 60

57. LITTLE GIRL, 1936
Drypoint, 8⅝ x 4⅝
Edition: 60

58. ROTHKO WITH A PIPE, 1936
Drypoint, 7⅛ x 6¾
Edition: 60
Reproduced in *Art in America,*
Vol. LI, No. 6, December, 1963,
p. 50

59. SELF-PORTRAIT, 1937
Drypoint, 7⅞ x 6⅜
Edition: 60
Reproduced in *Artist's Proof,* Vol. III,
No. 5, Spring–Summer, 1963, p. 29

60. MAN WITH PIPE, 1938
Drypoint, 6⅜ x 5¾
Edition: 60

21

61. JAPANESE LANDSCAPE, 1939
    Drypoint, 3⅛ x 7⅞
    Edition: 100

62. NUDE RECLINING, 1939
    Drypoint, 3⅝ x 7¼
    Edition: 60

63. ROSALIE, 1939
    Drypoint, 6⅜ x 4⅜
    Edition: 60

64. SALLY WITH BERET, 1939
    Drypoint, 7⅞ x 6⅜
    Edition: 100
    Reproduced in *Artist's Proof*, Vol. III,
        No. 5, Spring–Summer, 1963, p. 29

65. BATHERS, 1941
    Drypoint, 4¼ x 8½
    Edition: 60
    Reproduced in *Milton Avery.*
        Etchings and Woodcuts,
        Associated American Artists,
        1963, No. 15

66. HELEN AND LILLY, 1941
    Drypoint, 6¾ x 5¾
    Edition: 60

67. RECLINING NUDE, 1941
    Drypoint, 3½ x 7¼
    Edition: 100
    Reproduced in *Milton Avery.*
        Etchings and Woodcuts,
        Associated American Artists,
        1963, No. 16

68. STANDING NUDE, 1941
    Drypoint, 14¼ x 7⅝
    Edition: 60

69. WINDOW BY THE SEA, 1941
    Drypoint, 7⅜ x 4¾
    Edition: 60
    Reproduced in *Milton Avery.*
        Etchings and Woodcuts,
        Associated American Artists,
        1963, No. 17

70. TWISTED TREES, 1943
    Drypoint, 5 x 6¾
    Edition: 60

71. HEAD OF MARCH, 1948
    Also entitled *March with Babushka*
    Drypoint, 9⅝ x 9½
    Edition: 100, acquired by Collecto
        of American Art for distribution
        its membership in December, 194
    Reproduced in *The Art Digest,*
        Vol. XXIII, August 1, 1949, p. 1

72. LAURELS PORTFOLIO, No. 4,
    1948
    Five drypoint etchings on copper
        with an appreciation by Joseph
        Solman. Published by the Laurel
        Gallery. Printed by Stanley
        William Hayter at Atelier 17,
        New York, June, 1948.
    Edition: 100
    a. RIDERS IN THE PARK
        (1934) 3⅞ x 5
    b. HEAD OF A MAN
        (1935) 9 x 4¾
    c. RECLINING NUDE
        (1948) 6 x 15
    d. MARCH AT A TABLE
        (1948) 8¾ x 6
    e. BY THE SEA
        (1948) 4¾ x 7⅛
    The text and the title page were se
        and printed on the hand press o
        Douglass Howell on Howell hand
        made papers.

3. DAWN, 1952
   Woodcut, 7¼ x 9
   Black-and-white edition: 15
   Black-and-yellow edition: 100,
     acquired by Collectors of
     American Art for distribution
     to its membership

4. FISH, 1952
   Woodcut, 2¼ x 9
   Edition: 100

5. PILOT FISH, 1952
   Woodcut, 11⅜ x 30
   Black-and-white edition: 25
   Black-and-blue edition: 25

6. THREE BIRDS, 1952
   Woodcut, 9⅝ x 25
   Black-and-white edition: 15
   Black-and-yellow edition: 20
   Black-and-blue edition: 15
   Reproduced in *Milton Avery.*
     Etchings and Woodcuts,
     Associated American Artists,
     1963, No. 28

7. TWO BIRDS, 1952
   Woodcut, 2¾ x 6¾
   Black edition: 30
   Green edition: 20

8. FANCY BIRD, 1953
   Woodcut, 4½ x 6¾
   Black-and-white edition: 30
   Black-and-gold edition: 20

9. FANTAIL PIGEON, 1953
   Woodcut, 10 x 9⅝
   Black-and-white edition: 20
   Black-and-brown edition: 25
   Black-and-blue edition: 30
   Reproduced in *Milton Avery.*

Etchings and Woodcuts,
Associated American Artists,
1963, No. 32

80. FLIGHT, 1953
    Woodcut, 7¼ x 9
    Black-and-white edition: 20
    Black-and-blue edition: 25
    Black-and-brown edition: 100,
      acquired by Collectors of
      American Art for distribution to
      its membership

81. HOODED OWL, 1953
    Linoleum cut, 9 x 7
    Edition: 20

82. NIGHT NUDE, 1953
    Woodcut, 9¾ x 24
    Black-and-white edition: 25
    Black-and-blue edition: 20

83. NUDE, 1953
    Woodcut, 3⅝ x 10½
    Black-and-white edition: 20
    Black-and-blue edition: 20
    Grey edition: 25
    Green edition: 20
    Blue edition: 500, acquired by
      Art in America

84. ROOSTER, 1953
    Woodcut, 9⅝ x 7¼
    Black-and-white edition: 25
    Black-and-grey edition: 25
    Black-and-blue edition: 100,
      acquired by Collectors of
      American Art for distribution
      to its membership

85. SILLY HEN, 1953
    Woodcut, 9½ x 5¾
    Black-and-white edition: 30
    Black-and-yellow edition: 25

86. STRANGE BIRD, 1953
    Woodcut, 7¼ x 12¾
    Black-and-white edition: 20
    Black-and-yellow edition: 25

87. TREES BY THE SEA, 1953
    Woodcut, 9¾ x 13⅞
    Black-and-white edition: 20
    Brown-and-black edition: 20

88. BEACH BIRDS, 1954
    Woodcut, 7⅝ x 12
    Black-and-white edition: 25
    Blue edition: 25

89. DANCER, 1954
    Woodcut, 12 x 9⅝
    Black-and-white edition: 25
    Black-and-red edition: 25

90. HEN, 1954
    Woodcut, 12 x 9¾
    Black-and-white edition, 25
    Black-and-yellow edition: 20

91. LAMB, 1954
    Woodcut, 9⅝ x 13¾
    Black-and-white edition: 20
    Black-and-yellow edition: 20

Black-and-red edition: 20
Black-and-blue edition: 20
Note: After a painting, *Sheep*, 195?
    in the Collection of
    Mrs. Milton Avery

92. SAILBOAT, 1954
    Woodcut, 7½ x 12¼
    Edition: 25

93. BIRDS AND SEA, 1955
    Woodcut, 8⅜ x 24
    Black-and-white edition: 25
    Black-and-brown edition: 25
    Blue edition: 20

94. HEAD, 1955
    Woodcut, 12 x 9¾
    Edition: 25

95. NUDE COMBING HAIR, 1961
    Drypoint, 8½ x 6¹⁄₁₆
    Edition: 90

96. GRAY SEA, 1963
    Offset lithograph in color, 22 x 26¾
    Edition: 118
    Reproduced in *Art In America*,
        Vol. LII, No. 3, June, 1964, p. 10

Photographs of drawings and monotypes by Charles Uht
and of prints by Wolfgang Hartmann
except Plates 9 by O. E. Nelson an
29 by Geoffrey Clement

SLEEPING GIRL, 1930 (1)

THREE FIGURES, 1950 (6)

NUDE, 1953 (9)

SPOTTY TREES, 1956 (11)

TWO NUDES, 1956 (13)

ROUGH SEA, 1958 (19)

DUNE GRASSES, 1959 (21)

SELF-PORTRAIT, 1959 (22)

Milton Avery 1960.

:NDER DUNES, 1960 (23)

RECLINING NUDES, 1950 (37)

RECUMBENT NUDE, 1962 (24)

Greetings to my Dear friend Roy
On this his Birthday

Milton Avery

UNTITLED (Three Seated Nude Figures), n.d. (29)

LEAVES, 1951 (41)

SETTING SUN, 1951 (46)

MY WIFE SALLY, 1934 (53)

YOUNG GIRL NUDE, 1935 (54)

DRAWBRIDGE, 1936 (56)

ROTHKO WITH A PIPE, 1936 (58)

SELF-PORTRAIT, 1937 (59)

JAPANESE LANDSCAPE, 1939 (61)

MAN WITH PIPE, 1938 (60)

SALLY WITH BERET, 1939 (64)

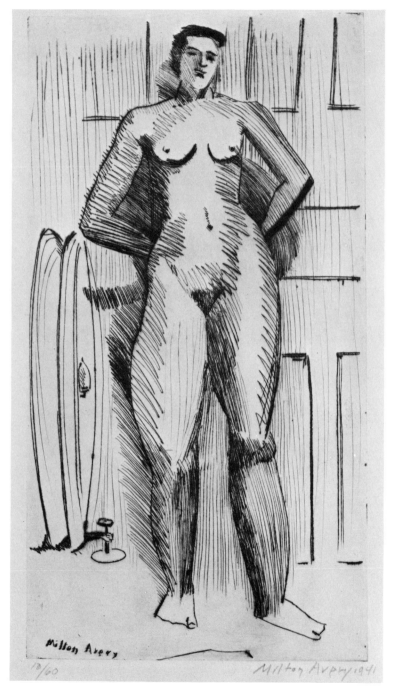

STANDING NUDE, 1941 (68)

WINDOW BY THE SEA, 1941 (69)

TWISTED TREES, 1943 (70)

HEAD OF MARCH, 1948 (71)

SOLITARY TREE, 1956 (50)

Milton Avery

artist proof

RIDERS IN THE PARK, 1934 (72a)

HEAD OF A MAN, 1935 (72b)

MARCH AT A TABLE, 1948 (72d)

BY THE SEA, 1948 (72e)

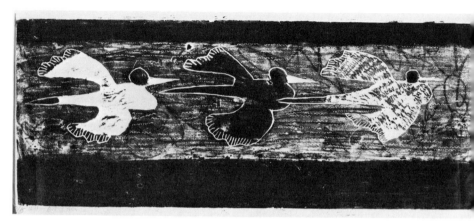

THREE BIRDS, 1952 (76)

FANTAIL PIGEON, 1953 (79)

HEN, 1954 (90)

LAMB, 1954 (91)

NUDE COMBING HAIR, 1961 (95)

CHRONOLOGY

1893   Born March 7, in Altmar, New York

1905   Moved with his family to Hartford, Connecticut

1913   Worked on night shift in Connecticut factory and painted outdoors during the day

1923   Enrolled in Connecticut League of Art Students

1925   Spent summer painting in Gloucester, Massachusetts. Moved to New York

1926   Married Sally Michel, painter and illustrator

1928   First exhibited at Opportunity Gallery, New York City

1929   Awarded the Logan Prize at the Art Institute of Chicago

1932   Daughter, March, was born

1935   First one-man exhibition at Valentine Gallery, New York City

1938   Spent summer on Gaspé Peninsula

1941   Worked in California

1946   Traveled in Mexico

1950   Winter in Florida

1952   First trip to Europe

1954   Summer in New Hampshire

1959   Won $1,000 award for *Sea and Dunes*

1965   Died January 3, New York City

AWARDS AND HONORS

1929   Art Institute of Chicago: Logan Prize for Watercolor

1930   Connecticut Academy of Fine Arts: Atheneum Prize

1949   Baltimore Watercolor Club: First Prize

1958   Boston Arts Festival: Second Prize

1959   Art USA 1959: $1,000 Award

1960   Ford Foundation Grant

ONE-MAN EXHIBITIONS

1928   Opportunity Gallery, New York City

1932   Gallery, 144 West 13th Street, New York City

1935   Valentine Gallery, New York City

1936   Valentine Gallery, New York City

1938   Valentine Gallery, New York City

1943   The Phillips Collection, Washington, D.C.
        Paul Rosenberg and Co., New York City

1944   The Arts Club of Chicago, Chicago, Illinois
        The Phillips Collection, Washington, D.C.
        Paul Rosenberg and Co., New York City
        Bertha Schaefer Gallery, New York City

62

1945   Durand-Ruel Galleries, New York City
        Paul Rosenberg and Co., New York City

1946   Paul Rosenberg and Co., New York City
        Durand-Ruel Galleries, New York City
        Colorado Springs Fine Arts Center, Colorado Springs, Colorado

1947   Durand-Ruel Galleries, New York City
        Portland Art Museum, Portland, Oregon

1949   Durand-Ruel Galleries, New York City

1950   Laurel Gallery, New York City (monotypes)
        Knoedler Gallery, New York City

1951   Grace Borgenicht Gallery, New York City

1952   Grace Borgenicht Gallery, New York City
        The Baltimore Museum of Art, Baltimore, Maryland (traveling
          retrospective exhibition)
        Joe and Emily Lowe Gallery, Coral Gables, Florida
        The Phillips Collection, Washington, D.C.
        Wadsworth Atheneum, Hartford, Connecticut

1953   The Institute of Contemporary Art, Boston, Massachusetts

1954   Grace Borgenicht Gallery, New York City
        H C E Gallery, Provincetown, Massachusetts
        University of Nebraska, Lincoln, Nebraska
        Santa Barbara Museum of Art, Santa Barbara, California

1956   Museum of Fine Arts of Houston, Houston, Texas
        Grace Borgenicht Gallery, New York City
        Mills College, Oakland, California
        Felix Landau Gallery, Los Angeles, California

1957   Grace Borgenicht Gallery, New York City
        Mills College, Oakland, California (drawings)

1958   Otto Seligman Gallery, Seattle, Washington
        H C E Gallery, Provincetown, Massachusetts
        Grace Borgenicht Gallery, New York City

1959	Felix Landau Gallery, Los Angeles, California
	H C E Gallery, Provincetown, Massachusetts
	Art Alliance, Philadelphia, Pennsylvania
1960	Whitney Museum of American Art, New York City
	(traveling retrospective exhibition sponsored by
	The American Federation of Arts under a
	Ford Foundation grant)
	Grace Borgenicht Gallery, New York City
1961	Shore Galleries, Boston, Massachusetts
	The Fort Wayne Art Museum, Fort Wayne, Indiana
1962	Park Gallery, Detroit, Michigan
	Makler Gallery, Philadelphia, Pennsylvania
	The Waddington Galleries, London, England
1963	Grace Borgenicht Gallery, New York City
	Associated American Artists, New York City
	(drypoints and woodcuts)
1964	Felix Landau Gallery, Los Angeles, California
	Donald Morris Gallery, Detroit, Michigan
1965	The Waddington Galleries, London, England
	The Phillips Collection, Washington, D.C.
	Richard Gray Gallery, Chicago, Illinois

GRAPHIC WORKS IN
PUBLIC COLLECTIONS

Addison Gallery of American Art, Phillips Academy,
Andover, Massachusetts

Albright-Knox Art Gallery, Buffalo, New York

The Baltimore Museum of Art, Baltimore, Maryland

Barnes Foundation, Merion, Pennsylvania

Brandeis University, Waltham, Massachusetts

The Brooklyn Museum, Brooklyn, New York

Bryn Mawr College, Bryn Mawr, Pennsylvania

The Butler Institute of American Art, Youngstown, Ohio

Dayton Art Institute, Dayton, Ohio

Evansville Museum of Arts and Sciences, Evansville, Indiana

Georgia Museum of Art, University of Georgia, Athens, Georgia

Honolulu Academy of Arts, Honolulu, Hawaii

The Metropolitan Museum of Art, New York City

Munson-Williams-Proctor Institute, Utica, New York

Museum of Fine Arts of Houston, Houston, Texas

The Museum of Modern Art, New York City

Nebraska Art Association, Lincoln, Nebraska

The Newark Museum, Newark, New Jersey

Norton Gallery, West Palm Beach, Florida

Pennsylvania Academy of the Fine Arts, Philadelphia, Pennsylvania

Philadelphia Museum of Art, Philadelphia, Pennsylvania

The Phillips Collection, Washington, D.C.

The Phillips Exeter Academy, Exeter, New Hampshire

Smith College Museum of Art, Northampton, Massachusetts

Tate Gallery, London, England

Tel Aviv Museum, Tel Aviv, Israel

University of Illinois, Champaign-Urbana, Illinois

University of Minnesota, Minneapolis, Minnesota

Walker Art Center, Minneapolis, Minnesota

Whitney Museum of American Art, New York City

Witte Memorial Museum, San Antonio, Texas

Yale University Art Gallery, New Haven, Connecticut

SELECTED BIBLIOGRAPHY

BOOKS AND PERIODICALS

Baker, Elizabeth C. "Milton Avery," *Art News*, LXII (October, 1963), p. 13

Breuning, Margaret. "Milton Avery," *The Art Digest*, XXV (December 15, 1950), p. 19

Frost, Rosamund. "Milton Avery, American Fauve," *Art News,* XLI (December 15, 1942), p. 28, 4 illus.

Gray, Cleve. "Print Review," *Art in America,* LI (December 1, 1963), p. 50, 1 illus.

Gray, Cleve. "Print Review," *Art in America,* LII (June, 1964), p. 104, 1 illus.

Greenberg, Clement. *Art and Culture — Critical Essays.* Boston, 1961, pp. 197–202

Guest, Barbara. "Avery and Gatch: Lonely Americans," *Art News,* LIX (March, 1960), pp. 42–45, 8 illus.

Kramer, Hilton. *Milton Avery: Paintings 1930–1960.* New York, 1962, 111 illus.

Lowengrund, Margaret. "Field of Graphic Arts" (column), *The Art Digest,* XXIII (August, 1949), p. 16, 1 illus.

Mullins, Edwin. "Developments in Style — XV: Milton Avery," *The London Magazine,* IV (January, 1965), pp. 34–40

Porter, Fairfield. "Milton Avery," *Art News,* LV (December, 1956), p. 10

"Printmaking: A Family Affair," *Artist's Proof,* V (Spring–Summer, 1963), p. 29, 4 illus.

Riley, Maude. "Milton Avery Fills an International Gap," *The Art Digest,* XIX (November 15, 1944), p. 10, 2 illus.

Ritter, Chris. "A Milton Avery Profile," *The Art Digest,* XXVII (December 1, 1952), pp. 11–12, 22, 1 illus.

Willard, Charlotte. "Drawing Today," *Art in America,* LII (October, 1964), p. 67, 1 illus.

Young, Vernon. "Milton Avery," *Arts,* XXXI (January, 1957), p. 50

EXHIBITION CATALOGUES

Baltimore, Maryland, Baltimore Museum of Art. *Milton Avery*, 1952, essay by Frederick S. Wight, 11 illus.

Chicago, Illinois, Richard Gray Gallery. *Milton Avery*, 1965, 7 illus.

Detroit, Michigan, Donald Morris Gallery. *Milton Avery*, 1964, 6 illus.

Detroit, Michigan, Park Gallery. *Paintings by Milton Avery*, 1962, 4 illus.

Houston, Texas, Museum of Fine Arts of Houston. *Milton Avery*, 1956, statement by the artist, 1 illus.

London, England, The Waddington Galleries. *Milton Avery*, 1962, essay by Clement Greenberg, 34 illus.

London, England, The Waddington Galleries. *Milton Avery*, 1965, 24 illus.

Los Angeles, California, Felix Landau Gallery. *Milton Avery*, 1956, 3 illus.

New York, New York, The American Federation of Arts. *Milton Avery*, 1960, catalogue by Adelyn Breeskin, 39 illus.

New York, New York, Associated American Artists. *Milton Avery. Etchings and Woodcuts*, 1963, text and catalogue by Sylvan Cole, Jr., 10 illus.

FILMS

A Painter's World. 16 mm. film about Avery, 14 minutes, produced by Walter Lewisohn Associates for the Americana Foundation, Inc.

The Americans — 3 East Coast Artists (Avery, Hofmann and Tworkov), filmed by Warren Forma